Wil Wong
and the
Sun Bear

by
Dr Sarah Pye

Wildlife Wong and the Sun Bear
February 2021

ISBN: 978-0-9806871-7-0 (paperback)
ISBN: 978-0-9806871-8-7 (ebook)

Published by:

Estralita Publishing
ABN: 86 230 144 690
P.O. Box 288
Buddina, QLD, 4575
⊕ www.sarahrpye.com

Pencil sketch illustrator: *Ali Beck*
Cover design: *Gram Telen*
Layout design: *Gram Telen*
Wildlife Wong cartoon illustrator: *Isuru Pltawala*
Cover sun bear photo: *Lin May Chiew, BSBCC*
Cover author photo: *Amber Grant*

 A catalogue record for this
work is available from the
NATIONAL LIBRARY OF AUSTRALIA   National Library of Australia

Check out what other kids think about this book...

"This is the best book I have ever read. I think lots of kids will love it and learn from it!"

India, Australia

"What I enjoyed most about the book was Damai's story. There was happiness and sadness. In my head, I could imagine what it would be like to be a sun bear."

Riley, Australia

"I like having the experiments at the end of the book because the experiments have to do with parts of the story, and it lets me become a scientist like Wong. I really hope other kids will love sun bears as much as I do after reading this book and help to save them like me."

Taylor, Canada

Hi, I am Wildlife Wong. This book is dedicated to you! Yes, that's right... by reading this book, you are helping me save sun bears!

I am Wong's friend Sarah,
and this is my dog Gypsy.
We live in Queensland which is
a state in Australia. Can you see
Queensland on this map?

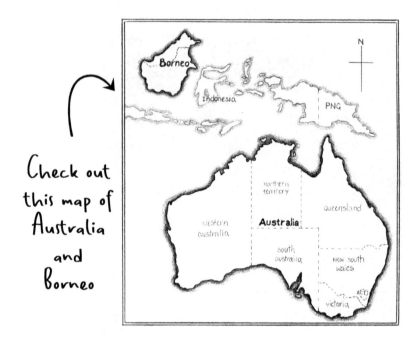

Check out this map of Australia and Borneo

I want to tell you a story about Wong, and *his* friend Damai (which sounds like 'dam eye'). Wong is a human being and Damai is a sun bear. Wong is an **ecologist** which means he is a scientist who studies how animals and plants live together. When you see a word beginning in 'eco' it means it has something to do with the environment. (Keep watch, you may see another word that starts with 'eco' a bit later.)

Wong and Damai in the rainforest

Wong and Damai live on an island called Borneo over 5,000km away from where I live. Can you see Borneo on the map?

How far is Borneo from where you live? (If you have a computer, why don't you find out?)

This book is different

This book includes cool stuff to do so you can be a scientist just like my friend Wong. It is also part of a series of books. I really enjoyed making this book, and I reckon you would enjoy making a book too. Do you want to make a book with me? If you go to my website, www.sarahrpye.com, you can download free pages for your own **Nature Journal** and a template for making an awesome cover.

Does that sound like fun? Then, let's begin with the story about Wong and Damai.

Damai is lost

One day, a man called Mr Lum heard a dog barking outside his house. He was busy watching television, so Mr Lum asked his son to go out and chase away the dog. His son couldn't believe what he saw. It wasn't a dog at all. It was a tiny, lonely sun bear cub barking for its mum. It is against the law to keep sun bears as pets, so they took the frightened bear inside and Mr Lum called the police. Soon, wildlife experts came with a small cage. They took the tiny sun bear to Wildlife Wong who is an expert in taking care of bears. He runs a very special place called the Bornean Sun Bear Conservation Centre. Wong looks after about forty bears. All of them have been rescued — some from private houses, and others from cramped zoos.

It must be scary in a small cage

PHOTOGRAPH: © BSBCC

Damai meets Wong

When Wong first saw the cub, her nose, or **muzzle**, looked too big for her body. He thought it was so big, she might fall over. Her smile was turned down at the edges, which made her look very sad. Her big, round puppy-like eyes made him want to comfort her.

He put his fingers through the cage, and she sucked on them like a human baby sucking her thumb. When he lifted her up, the cub was very light, and she snuggled into his shoulder.

Wong could see a gold shape on her chest, called a **ventral patch**, when he tickled her stomach. It looked like a thin horseshoe. Wong knew a horseshoe is supposed to be lucky. He thought the cub was unlucky because she had lost her mum, but she was lucky she was now finally safe.

He decided he would have to be her new mum, but baby sun bears need a lot of care, so bear keeper Lin May would help. First, the cub needed a name. Wong called her Damai, after the town where Mr Lum lived. It seemed like a good name because Damai means 'peace' in the Malay language.

My name, Sarah, means 'princess'.
Do you know what your name means?
If you do, put it on the front of your Nature Journal.

Damai had to be kept **in isolation** away from other bears for a month because Wong wanted to make sure she didn't have any germs that would harm the other bears. Have you ever had to be in isolation to keep yourself or other people safe?

Damai was very hungry. She was given a bottle of milk every four hours and she soon grew strong. Sometimes Lin May gave her a honey treat from a squeeze bottle. Honey was her favourite.

Damai drinking milk from a baby bottle

Meeting the other bears

After four weeks in isolation, it was time to introduce Damai to the other bears. She was moved to a den in the noisy bear house with the other forty bears. The den was much bigger than the cage in isolation.

There were strong metal bars between each den which kept her safe. A metal basket on the wall was lined with sweet-smelling pandanus leaves for sitting in. Pandanus leaves (which sounds like pan-dan-us) are sometimes used in cooking. There was also a sink in the corner and a real tree branch was suspended across the den like a swing. There were metal sliding doors between the dens, and one at the far end. All of them were locked shut.

Damai could see the other bears climbing up their bars to look at her. They looked a bit like her mum, but they weren't as friendly. When they barked, she was scared. Damai curled into the wall basket to hide, but slowly, she became curious.

Eventually, she climbed up the bars to get a better look at the other bears. As long as they stayed where they were, she felt brave. Damai grabbed the rope and swung on the branch in delight. Wong giggled as he watched.

Learning to be a sun bear

As Damai's new mums, Wong and Lin May needed to teach her wild bear skills. She needed to learn to dig for tasty **termites**, climb trees, and protect herself from other animals and humans. They took her out of her den every day. Damai followed Wong down the concrete path like his shadow and they went to the forest.

Wong sat down on the crunchy leaves and leaned against a tree while Damai explored. Sun bears have a very good sense of smell, just like dogs. Damai crinkled her nose and followed the smell of termites to a dead tree stump. She ripped the wood apart with her teeth and claws until she found tasty termites.

Damai was a clever bear. When her belly was full, she walked over to a small tree with vines wrapped around it. She used the vines as steps and climbed up high. She found a place where a branch met the trunk and sat with her legs dangling down. She was very pleased with herself, and Wong was too. She was learning her lessons well.

Damai climbed high into the tree

Do you like climbing trees like Damai? Maybe you have a photo you can stick in your Nature Journal, or you can draw a picture?

One day, Damai was rolling in dry leaves and throwing them in the air when she heard the crack of branches. Instantly, she stopped. If Damai's real mum was there, she would have jumped in front of her to protect her from danger, but Damai didn't have her mum.

The leaves in the next tree were moving, and something was coming towards her.

She stood up as tall as she could, and huffed a warning bark. She hoped it would scare away whatever made the noise. Then she saw a flash of orange. It was a mother **orangutan** swinging towards her with her baby holding on tight. Orangutans are one of our closest relatives and the word orangutan (which sounds like orang-oo-tan) even means 'man of the forest'. Isn't it funny that their name almost tells you what colour they are?

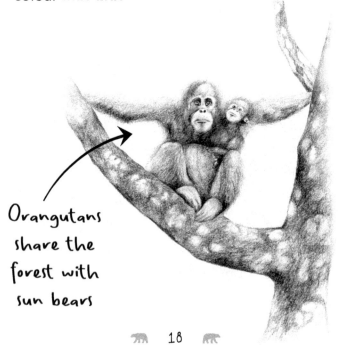

Orangutans share the forest with sun bears

Damai was scared but she tried to look even bigger by stretching out her arms. She barked as loud as she could. Then she turned around quickly and climbed the nearest tree as fast as she could move, hiding in the branches. She stayed as still as possible until the intruders had gone. That was close!

All of a sudden Damai was tired. She curled up and went to sleep. Wong waited below. When she woke up, he called her down. Together they walked back to the bear house. It had been an important day. Damai was learning to protect herself.

Can you imagine taking a sun bear for a walk?

PHOTOGRAPH: © BSBCC

Making new friends

When Damai was nearly one year old, she weighed almost twenty kilos. That is probably about how much you weighed when you were six. She was also getting much stronger. Wong knew if Damai got angry she could hurt him by mistake, so he couldn't take her to the forest anymore. It was time for her to make friends with three other sun bear cubs called Mary, Debbie and Fulung (which sounds like 'full-long').

One by one, the sliding doors between dens were opened. Damai didn't really like Mary so she ignored her. Damai didn't really like Debbie either. But when Fulung came into her den, they became instant friends. They rolled across the concrete floor together playing. Debbie and Mary were happy to climb up into the basket and watched the fun.

Damai and her
new friend Fulung

Damai found it hard work making friends, and she soon got hot and tired. She wandered to the sink in the corner of her den and splashed herself with water to cool off. Wong smiled as he watched her. He was glad she was no longer alone.

Learning about electricity

Damai and her new friends were introduced to three more bears – Koko, Bongkud (which sounds like bong-could) and Ah Bui (which sounds like ahh-boy). They now had a bear cub gang. Each day was more fun than the last. They chased each other up the bars and cuddled together while they slept.

They didn't know that on the other side of one of the metal sliding doors was a huge natural playground, or forest enclosure. Wong wanted to let Damai and her friends go through the door before they forgot how to climb trees but there was still one more step they had to take before they could explore.

The enclosure was surrounded by a very tall fence to keep the bears in and the people out. There was electricity flowing through the wires. If a bear touched the wire, they would get a shock. It wasn't enough to kill them, but it would hurt, just like if you touched a hot stove by mistake.

Before the bear friends could be let out in the forest enclosure, they were taken to the training pen which was a small square area surrounded by wire. The electricity running through the fences in the training pen was not as powerful as in the forest enclosure. It was designed to sting and scare the young bears, so they learnt to stay away.

This is the sun bear gang

PHOTOGRAPH: © BSBCC

Wong dribbled honey very close to the wire, then opened the door to Damai's den. She followed the smell of her favourite treat. As she reached for the honey, her back touched the wire. She thought a bee had stung her. She turned around and ran back into her den as quick as she could and tried to lick herself better. Have you ever been stung by a bee? What did you do?

Over the next two weeks, the same training was repeated four more times. When Wong felt the bear gang had learnt the lesson, he opened the doors between their pens and the forest. Damai stood on the edge of the wooden ramp with her paws outside in the sunlight. She stared out at the forest. She was finally free to explore, but the world looked so big!

Bongkud ran out and climbed a tree. Ah Bui found a fallen tree log and stretched out in the sun. Wong threw coconuts over the fence and Fulung grabbed one under his arm, like a football player. He ran to the base of the big tree and leaned against it while he sunk his black claws into the husk and pulled it apart in seconds. He then rolled onto his back and balanced the coconut on his four paws so he could lick the dripping coconut water.

Have you ever tasted coconut water? What did it taste like?

Yum...
coconuts!

PHOTOGRAPH: © BSBCC

A storm in the forest

One day, the sky grew very dark. Damai could sense a storm coming. She could smell the rain and wanted to climb higher before it started. She didn't like it when sticky mud squashed between her toes.

Suddenly, a wind came out of nowhere, crashing branches together. Then a powerful lightning bolt struck, and the ground shook. Damai ran as fast as she could towards the bear house. She would be safe there. Three of her friends ran fast behind her but Bongkud was still high at the top of a tree.

Another noisy lightning bolt lit up the sky. It hit the top of Bongkud's tree and moved instantly through her body to the ground. The amount of electricity was a hundred times more powerful than the electric fence and it killed Bongkud. The tree splintered into tiny strips and Bongkud fell down, down, down until she hit the ground.

Wong was very sad because he loved Bongkud. He also wanted to release Damai back into the wild one day, but he was reminded that the life of a wild bear is dangerous. He needed to make sure she had as many skills as possible first.

The next day, the bears weren't allowed to go outside. Wong and his team cut up the tree with chain saws and took it away. Then they checked that the electric fence was not damaged.

Damai missed her friend, but life for the rest of the sun bear gang slowly returned to normal. One day, close to Damai's first birthday, she walked slowly to her favourite tree and started to climb. Instead of napping on a comfortable branch like she had so many times, Damai bent the thin branches in her mouth until she had made her first ever nest. She lined her nest with leaves and snuggled into it for the rest of the day.

Can you see the sun bear on her nest?

PHOTOGRAPH: © BSBCC

Wong was excited. If Damai could make a nest, he knew that one day soon she would be able to go back to the forest and be a wild bear. He started looking for the perfect place.

Damai's new home needed to be as safe as possible. It needed to be far away from the poachers who had killed her mum. Wong settled on a place called Tabin Wildlife Reserve. It was very large, there was plenty of food, and it was **illegal** to hunt animals there (which means it is against the law). Can you find Tabin on the Borneo map?

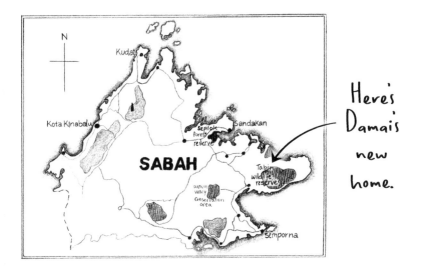

Here's Damai's new home.

Putting on a collar

Wong wanted to be able to track Damai once she was free. He couldn't use Snapchat or Google because Tabin was out of phone range, so Wong needed to fit Damai with a collar containing a **satellite transmitter**. This amazing device sends information up to a satellite circling the earth. The satellite sends a signal back down to a country on the other side of the world called Germany. Then people in Germany email Wong the collar's location every few days.

You can't just walk up to a sun bear and ask them to stand still while you put a collar around their neck. Damai was put to sleep like you would be if you needed an operation. Then Wong wrapped the heavy collar around her neck and fastened it with bolts so Damai couldn't break it off. Over the next few weeks, the collar worked well. Wong could see where she was going around the rainforest enclosure.

Wong could track Damai using her collar

PHOTOGRAPH: © BSBCC

One last sleep

I asked Wong if I could help release Damai, and he said yes, so I got on an airplane and flew from Australia to Malaysia. As dark fell the day before Damai would be free, the noisy cicadas (which sounds like sa-car-das) quietened down for the night. Cicadas are insects that look like moths with **transparent** (or see-through) wings.

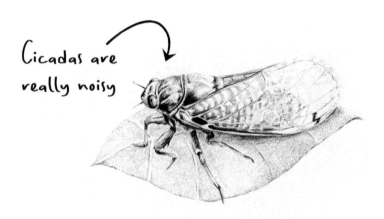

Cicadas are really noisy

I watched the animal doctor, or **veterinarian**, Dr Nabila, approach Damai's cage. She wore black boots, a black shirt and black **hijab**, or head covering. She looked just like a ninja warrior.

Dr Nabila was going to **sedate** Damai, which means making her go to sleep, so she could be moved to a travelling cage. Dr Nabila looked at the time on her oversized watch then raised the dart gun and aimed it at Damai. Damai sensed danger so she tried to escape by climbing, but Dr Nabila pulled the trigger and the dart hit Damai in the back. Damai reached back with her left arm and pulled it out.

Suddenly, the bulky collar around her neck felt very heavy so she climbed down. She shook her head to try and stay awake, but it was no use. Her tongue hung from her mouth and she tried to lick her dry lips. Before long, she was asleep on the concrete floor.

Wong and his friends quickly lifted her onto the operating table. Damai lay on her stomach with her legs stretched out like a rug. I moved closer to take a look. I had never been this close to a sun bear before. Her teeth were sharp, her claws were bent, and the soles of her paws were pink.

Everyone was very busy. Someone measured her arms, legs, head and paws and wrote the results on a clipboard. They then put her paws on an inkpad and made a paw print. Someone else put a thermometer up her bottom to record her temperature. They cut off a small handful of her fur and put it in an envelope. It would be used to test her DNA. DNA is like the recipe which makes up a life and Wong could use it to tell him what other bears she was related to.

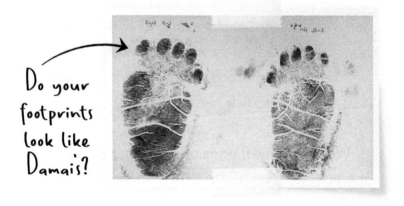

Do your footprints look like Damai's?

Then four men carried Damai outside and put her inside a small cage called a **translocation** cage. The word 'translocation' means moving from one place to another. It was a small cage which measured only one metre wide and two metres long (3 feet wide and 6 feet long). If you have a measuring tape, why don't you measure a square on the floor and see if you can lie down inside it?

The sun was nearly gone, and the shadows were long and creepy. It was time for the humans to get some sleep.

The journey begins

When she woke up with a headache, Damai was lying on a soft bed of leaves. She could barely turn around. Time had disappeared but Damai knew it was the middle of the night because she could hear frogs croaking.

At 2am, Wong knocked on my bedroom door and I got dressed quickly. I hadn't slept much because I was excited. We drove back to the bear house and he walked straight to Damai's cage. Wong stuck the end of a bottle of water through the bars and Damai drank in big gulps. Then he squeezed honey on the bars of her cage as a treat. Four tired men lifted her cage into the back of a truck and slammed the tailgate. Wong got into the driver's seat and I got into the back. The doors clunked shut. Operation 'Freedom' had begun.

Travelling to her new home

We drove south for five hours through the cool night to the edge of Tabin Wildlife Reserve. As the sun came up and the sky turned orange, we reached the gate to the reserve. Two wild bearded pigs ran across the road, and a hawk-eagle stood on the fence post welcoming us.

A ride in a helicopter

As the sun rose, so did the heat. We couldn't drive any further because there were no roads into the middle of the reserve. The last part of the journey would take place by helicopter.

Wong and his helpers lifted Damai's cage down from the truck. They placed it next to a concrete pad painted with a huge yellow H. This was the helicopter landing zone. Then we waited. We heard the repeating thud of the blades before the helicopter appeared over the treetops. As it came down and landed before us, dry grass blew up Damai's twitching nose.

First, the release team, in their black sun bear T shirts and black rubber boots, were flown to the release site to get ready. Wong and I were on the second helicopter trip. Have you ever flown in a helicopter? I was nervous.

This is me flying Damai to her new home

Wong jumped in the back and I climbed into the front seat next to the pilot. It was very noisy, so the pilot told me to put on the headphones. Voices through the headphones sounded like they were a long way off.

Below my feet, the bottom of the helicopter was glass. I watched the ground move away as the helicopter rose. It moved forward over Damai's cage which was wrapped in a thick **cargo net**.

A man wearing huge earmuffs directed the pilot into position, then he connected a cable from the net to the bottom of the helicopter. When he was ready, he waved us off, and the helicopter rose like a dragonfly. Damai's cage swung below. What do you think Damai was thinking?

Wong had his gum boots on

We flew over the treetops for fifteen minutes. It looked like a bunch of broccoli below us. Then a grey bald spot appeared between the trees. We were right in the middle of the reserve, at a mud volcano. It wasn't like a fiery volcano you may be imagining. In a mud volcano, salty mud oozes from underground. It smells a bit like rotten eggs. The mud volcano was the only possible landing area in the rainforest.

The pilot hovered, then landed Damai's cage on the muddy crust. A man from the first helicopter trip unhooked the net, then the pilot landed softly. As I climbed down, I stepped into a huge elephant footprint. It was twice as long as my foot. I quickly looked around, but the elephant had gone. Elephants love the volcano because they like to lick the tasty, salty mud.

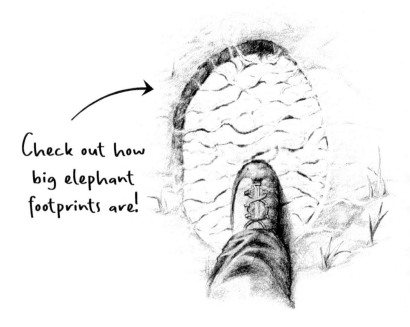

Check out how big elephant footprints are!

Saying goodbye

Wong moved to one corner of the cage. He counted to three and lifted it up with three other men. They moved together and squelched through the mud to the edge of the forest. Then they placed the cage down in the cool forest on soft fallen leaves.

Wong walked around looking up at the strong trees. He kicked the leaves, and a pill **millipede** (which sounds like milly-peed) curled into a protective ball. 'Milli' means thousand and 'pede' means legs. Millipedes don't really have a thousand legs, but they have more than you can count, and that's how they got their name. Wong smiled. Sun bears love crunchy millipedes. It looked like a good place for Damai to call home.

The release team had placed a camera on a tripod to record the beginning of Damai's new life. The time had come for her to be free. He crouched down beside Damai's cage to say goodbye. "You are back where you belong, Damai," he said, "I kept my promise."

Wong said his final goodbye to Damai

PHOTOGRAPH: © BSBCC

Wong leaned against a tree, holding the end of a long rope in both his hands. The other end was attached to the door of Damai's cage. I stood farther away with my heart pounding in my chest.

At exactly 10.45am, Wong tugged on the rope. The door fell away and Damai walked slowly out of the cage. She stood tall on her back legs and sniffed the humid, muddy air. She could also smell honey she had been unable to reach, so she turned around and licked it off the metal bars. Then she saw the funny black box on a tripod and walked over to investigate.

Damai smudged the GoPro camera lens with her honey breath and it filmed her nostrils. I giggled. Damai heard me. She turned and walked in my direction. I ran. She may be cute, but Damai was a wild animal. I did not want her to get too close. As my boots sunk into the mud, Damai stopped and turned away. Within seconds, she was gone.

Damai
was free!

Have you ever felt sad and happy at the same time?

That's how Wong felt. He was sad — like a mum who was never going to see her baby again. He was also happy because Damai was free and he knew that wild animals belong back in the wild. As he climbed back into the helicopter, he glanced over his shoulder and tried to take a picture in his mind to remember this moment.

As we flew back over Damai's new home, Wong began planning the future. There were many other sun bears who needed his help, and many other rainforest creatures that needed a home.

Want to know more about sun bears?

Did you enjoy that story? Now, why don't we learn a bit more about sun bears and their **habitat** (where they live). THEN, it's your turn to become a scientist!

The smallest bear in the world

There are eight different species of bears in the world. Here's a picture of them. Can you name any of them? (Hint: Koalas are NOT bears!) Sun bears are the smallest of the world's eight bear species. They are about the same size as a big dog.

What do sun bears look like?

Sun bears have a very long tongue. Sometimes it is as long as 33centimetres (13 inches) which is longer than a ruler. It's also more than twice as long as your tongue. Can you imagine that?

Sun bears have strong, pointed, curved claws which help them dig for food and climb really high in the trees. Sun bears have thick black **fur** and tiny round ears. They have a gold muzzle or nose which looks like they dipped it in honey.

The gold shape on a sun bear's chest is called a ventral patch. It is different on each bear, just like your fingerprints are different from everyone else's.

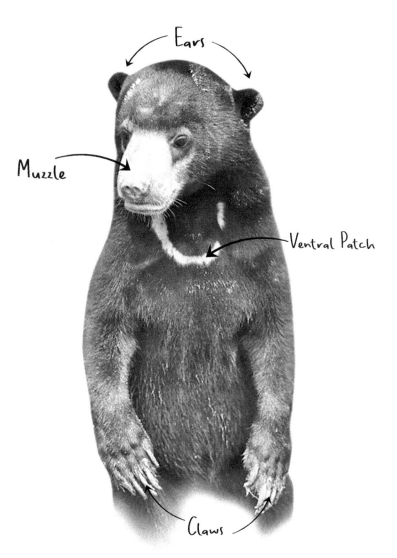

Ears

Muzzle

Ventral Patch

Claws

What do sun bears eat?

Sun bears eat all kinds of things. The word for animals that eat other animals and plants is an **omnivore** (which sounds like om- nee- vor). **Omni** means 'all things' and vore means 'animal that eats'. Sun bears have three favourite foods: honey, termites and wild figs. To find honey, sun bears climb in the trees as high as Godzilla (yes really!). They are looking for bee nests in the tree hollows. When they find a nest, they dig out the honey with their long claws and lick up every drop with their long tongues.

They also use their claws to break apart pieces of wood, searching for big ants called termites that bore tunnels through wood and eat it as they go. When the sun bears find termites they catch them on their long, sticky tongues and quickly eat them before they fall off. I wonder if it tickles?

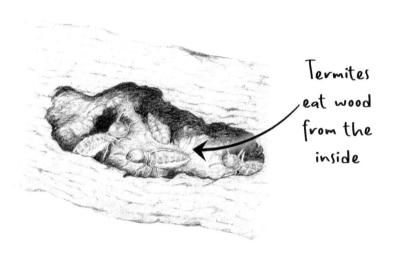

Termites eat wood from the inside

Sun bears love fruit too and their favourite wild fruit is figs. Have you ever eaten a fig? The ones in the rainforest are much smaller than the ones we are used to. Figs grow high in trees and sun bears need to climb high to pick them. What are your favourite three things to eat? Are you an omnivore? Perhaps you are a **herbivore**, because you only eat plants? Or a **carnivore**, because you only eat meat?

Sun bears are an important part of the rainforest **ecosystem**. I told you we would have another word that started with 'eco' ☺. An ecosystem is like a community of living things that live and work together. When sun bears poo, they spread seeds which grow into new trees. When they dig out bee hollows to eat the honey, birds move in to make a new home. When they lick up termites, they protect the trees from being eaten. If there were no sun bears, many other creatures, and trees, would suffer.

Hornbills
make
homes in
hollows

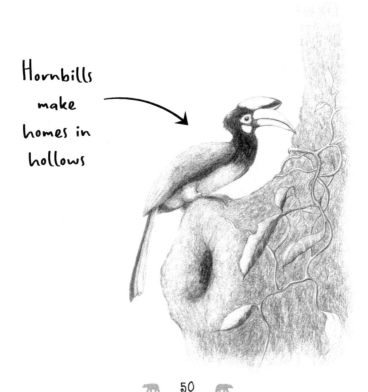

Why are sun bears in danger?

This part is really sad. There are not many sun bears left in the forest. One day soon, sun bears might be extinct because people cut down the forest and they have nowhere to live.

Some people also trap bears, then kill them and cut them into pieces to sell or eat. Killing sun bears is illegal but some sun bear parts are worth a lot of money, so some people kill them and hope they won't get caught. These people are called **poachers**.

If poachers kill a mother bear, they sometimes capture her baby and sell it as a pet. Just like puppies, sun bears are cute when they are small, but sun bears grow up to be dangerous animals. Wong is trying to save sun bears from **extinction**. Extinction means there are none of that animal left. Perhaps you have heard that dinosaurs are **extinct**. They were wiped out a very long time ago. Unfortunately, animals are becoming extinct all the time. Experts say there are about 200 species that become extinct every year. Scientist, like Wong, are trying their best to save animals from extinction. Being a scientist is a very important job, don't you think?

Let's save sun bears together!

PHOTOGRAPH: © BSBCC

Next time, I will tell you all about *Wildlife Wong and the Orangutan*! But first, do you want to do some experiments, and become a scientist?

Experiment 1
Can you make electricity?

The fences around the rainforest pens at the Bornean Sun Bear Conservation Centre have electricity moving through them. Electricity powers your lights at home. It is also stored in batteries which power some of your appliances and games. The electricity in a battery is generated by a chemical reaction between two **electrodes** made of copper and zinc, and an **electrolyte** liquid. Electrolyte liquid can come from a number of different places, even potatoes. Do you want to make electricity from a potato?

You will need:

6-8 potatoes

6-8 copper 'arms' (use copper screws, or nails, or even old copper pipe)

6-8 zinc 'arms' (galvanised 'clout' roofing nails are perfect... but you may find something else made of zinc)

14 pieces of thin electrical wire about 10-15 centimetres (6 inches) long with the ends stripped so you can see the copper strands

A small LED light (red or white is best because it uses the lowest voltage)

A 100 Ohm LED resistor (or a number close to that)

Paper and glue (or tape) if you want to make faces on your potatoes like I did...

An old, flat piece of wood or a tray big enough to put your experiment on

* If you haven't got all the ingredients, check out the experiments packs in the Wildlife Wong Kids' Club at www.sarahrpye.com

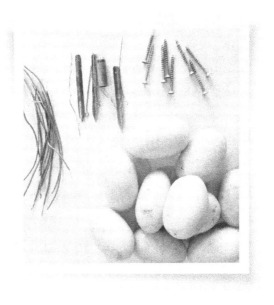

Steps:
(Check out the video at www.sarahrpye.com)

1. Twist the end of one piece of electrical wire to the long wire leg on the **LED**.
2. Twist the other end of the same electrical wire to one end of the **resistor**.

3. Twist another piece of electrical wire to the other end of the resistor.

4. Twist another piece of electrical wire onto the short leg of the LED.

5. Put that aside for a while to work on your potatoes.

6. Cut the bottom off your potatoes so they stand up on the wood.

7. Decorate them with Mr Potato Head faces or draw faces on if you like! (This doesn't make more electricity, but it makes it more fun!)

8. Screw or push the arms into the potatoes. Each Mr Potato Head should have one copper arm and one zinc arm. Zinc is grey and copper is orange-gold colour.

9. Stand your Mr Potato Heads in a circle. The copper arm on one Mr Potato Head should be next to the zinc arm on the next one.

10. Twist a piece of wire around the first potato's copper arm. It doesn't matter what colour the wire is.

11. Twist the other end of the same wire around the second potato's zinc arm.

12. Continue doing this until you have six Mr Potato Heads making a big circle. It should look like they are all holding hands, but with one gap in the circle.

13. Now pick up your LED with the wires attached.

14. Twist the wire which is connected to the resistor to the last copper arm.

15. Twist the wire which is connected to the short end of the LED to the last zinc arm, making the circle complete.

Does your light bulb go on?

Trouble shooting

If the light doesn't turn on, try adding another potato in the series to make more power or **voltage**.

If you have a regular light bulb, it needs much more voltage to make it light, so you will need a lot more potatoes!

How does it work?

You have just created an electrical series. That means the power generated in one potato is added to the power generated in the next potato. The more potatoes you have in the series, the more electricity, or voltage, is produced. Each potato produces around 0.84 volts. You will need about 5 volts in the series to light up the LED. That's why you need about six potatoes.

Guess what?

If you boil the potatoes first, it reduces the internal resistance, which increases the voltage.

Lemons and oranges work really well with this experiment too. You can even use a bunch of bananas…

If you produce enough electricity, you can even charge your mobile phone. But that's an experiment for another day!

Experiment 2
Animals get bored too!

The sun bears at the Bornean Sun Bear Conservation Centre play in the rainforest all day. They come back to the bear house at about 4pm for their dinner. The bear keepers make toys for them, so they don't get bored in the evening. These toys are called **enrichments**.

This sun bear really loves her present!

Photograph: © BSBCC

Every bear gets a present. Some of them figure it out quickly, but some take a long time to work out how to get to the peanut butter!

ANY animal who is left alone can get bored. Can you make an enrichment for your pet, or your friend's pet? If you don't know anyone with a pet, how about making them for animals in the shelter? Note: You should watch over your pet when you give them a new toy until you know they won't hurt themselves.

Cat Octopus

You will need:

An empty cardboard toilet roll

A pair of scissors

Felt tip pens to decorate

A hole punch

Ribbon, string or wool

Steps:
(Check out the video at www.sarahrpye.com)

1. Snip into the end of the toilet roll about half way

2. Do the same every 2-3 centimetres (1 inch) around the circle

3. Fan out your octopus's legs

4. Draw or paint a face on the top section

5. Fold the top together so you can make two holes with the hole punch at the same time

6. Cut about 1-2 metres (6 feet) of ribbon, string or wool

7. Thread the ribbon, string or wool through the two holes and tie it together into a loop

8. Hold the loop and jump the octopus around in front of your cat!

Magic cat wand

You will need:

An old shoelace

A stick from a tree, or a chopstick

A cardboard cereal box or scraps of felt

A hole puncher and/or scissors

Steps:
(Check out the video at www.sarahrpye.com)

1. Cut random shapes out of the cereal box or felt. The more colourful the better!
2. Punch a hole, or cut a hole, in the middle of each
3. Tie the end of the shoestring into a big knot, or tie it around one of the shapes
4. Thread the other end through the rest of the shapes
5. Tie the loose end of the shoestring around the stick or chopstick
6. Wave the wand in the air so the cat jumps up to catch the shapes!

Dog vending machine

My dog eats her dinner in about thirty seconds. This enrichment means it take a little longer, and she has to use her brain to shake the vending machine! This enrichment isn't suitable for big dogs though, because they just bite the bottle and they may hurt themselves!

You will need:

A strong plastic bottle
Dried dog food

Steps:
(Check out the video at www.sarahrpye.com)

1. Half fill the bottle with dog food
2. Shake this toy, then put it on the floor when you go out. Your dog will keep busy trying to release their dinner!

Dog popsicle

Do you like a cold popsicle on a hot day? So does your dog!

You will need:

A rawhide dog chew or dental chew

A plastic cup

Small dog food morsels (this can be anything from chicken bits to corn kernels!)

Steps:
(Check out the video at www.sarahrpye.com)

1. Fill the plastic cup loosely with small dog treats
2. Push the rawhide treat into the cup so it stands up like a popsicle stick
3. Fill the cup to the top with fresh water
4. Carefully stand the cup in the freezer until it is solid ice
5. When you are ready to give the popsicle to your dog, run the cup under warm water for a few seconds to release it
6. If your dog is trained, see if you can make them sit before handing it over!

New words

Some of the words or phrases in this book are bold. Here's what they mean. They are in alphabetical order. If a word (or phrase) starts with A, AN or THE, it is a noun (a person, place or thing). If it starts with TO BE, it is a verb (a doing word). An adverb describes (or adds to) a verb, and an adjective describes (or adds to) a noun. I reckon it should be called an adnoun!

A **cargo net** — A net which is really thick and heavy for carrying very heavy boxes and cages.

A **carnivore** — an animal that only (or mostly) eats meat.

An **ecologist** — a person who studies how animals and plants work together.

An **ecosystem** — all the animals and plants that work together in a habitat.

An **electrode** — solid electric conductor that carries electric current.

An **electrolyte** — a substance that conducts electricity.

An **enrichment** — a toy which improves an animal's life.

Extinct — an adjective which describes a species which is no longer alive.

An **extinction** — a happening which kills the last of a species.

A **habitat** — the natural home environment of an animal.

A **herbivore** — an animal that only eats plants.

A **hijab** — a scarf worn by a Muslim woman to cover her hair and neck.

Humid — an adjective which describes hot, wet air.

Illegal — an adjective which describes something which is against the law.

Isolation — a place away from other people (or bears!).

An **LED** — **Light emitting diode**. A very efficient type of light bulb.

A **millipede** — an insect with a hard shell and lots of legs.

A **muzzle** — The nose of an animal.

A **nature diary** — a special book where you record things you see, hear and find. You can download your own Nature Journal pages and a cover template at **sarahrpye.com**

An **omnivore** — an animal that eats both plants and other animals.

An **orangutan** — an ape that lives in the rainforest in Borneo and swings in the trees.

The **oxygen** — a gas you can't see, but people breathe it to live.

The **poachers** — people who catch and kill animals illegally.

The **precipitation** — rain, hail or snow.

A **resistor** — a small device which slows electricity moving through a wire.

A **satellite** — a man-made object which revolves around the earth.

A **termite** — small ant in the rainforest which eats wood.

Translocation — changing location. This word describes the cage, so it is an adjective.

A **transmitter** — an electrical device which sends a signal.

Transparent — an adjective which describes something you can see through.

A **ventral patch** — the gold horseshoe shape on a sun bear's chest.

A **voltage** — measure of electrical force. It is measured in numbers. The bigger the number, the more electricity.

Do you want to read more?

Wildlife Wong is lucky. He has adventures will all kinds of animals!

Why not check out these stories next?

Do you want to help sun bears?

Here are a few ideas:

- Lend this book to your friends so they can learn about sun bears too
- Do a school project on sun bears
- Adopt a sun bear with your family or your class at www.bsbcc.my
- Join the Wildlife Wong Kids' Club and download your free Nature Journal at www.sarahrpye.com
- If you waste less and buy less, less rainforest needs to be cut down
- Volunteer with a conservation group in your own area – the entire environment needs help, not just sun bears!

- If you are old enough, connect with me on Instagram or Facebook
- Send me an email at www.sarahrpye.com to share more ideas!

For teachers and parents:

Sarah Pye is available for speaking engagements, keynote addresses, and workshops online and in person. For more information, visit:

⊕ **www.sarahrpye.com**

This book is printed on demand (POD) which reduces waste and saves our trees.

Lightning Source UK Ltd.
Milton Keynes UK
UKHW021122100521
383452UK00004B/80